Pentatonic Scales

FOR GUITAR

BY CHAD JOHNSON

To access audio visit:
www.halleonard.com/mylibrary
Enter Code
7293-5871-4798-6481

ISBN 978-0-634-04646-9

HAL•LEONARD®
CORPORATION

7777 W. BLUEMOUND RD. P.O. BOX 13819 MILWAUKEE, WI 53213

In Australia Contact:
Hal Leonard Australia Pty. Ltd.
22 Taunton Drive P.O. Box 5130
Cheltenham East, 3192   Victoria, Australia
Email: **ausadmin@halleonard.com**

Visit Hal Leonard Online at
www.halleonard.com

Table of Contents

Introduction

If there were a "desert island" scale for the guitarist, you can bet it would most likely be the pentatonic scale. Without question, it is the most frequently heard scale in most guitar-dominated genres, including rock, blues, metal, country, and funk, to name a few. You'd be hard pressed to find a solo in any one of these styles that didn't have at least a few pentatonic licks at some point, and you can rest assured that this isn't likely to change any time in the near future. Ever since the birth of rock 'n' roll in the early fifties, the pentatonic scale and the guitar have been practically attached at the hip. Records by Chuck Berry, the Beach Boys, the Everly Brothers, Elvis, and countless others spilled over with pentatonic guitar licks, initiating a trend that has yet to go out of style.

So what is it about this scale that guitarists find so attractive? One aspect of its allure would certainly have to be attributed to the fact that it's so easy to play on the instrument. Fingerings of pentatonic scales on the guitar generally lay out very neatly, largely due to the way a guitar is tuned. The notes of the scale form visual patterns on the neck of a guitar that are easily learned and transposed all over the neck. Since guitarists generally come from untrained musical backgrounds, we appreciate the efficiency and simplicity this affords.

All of this is not to say that the reason guitarists love pentatonic scales is that we're too stupid or lazy to learn anything else. The simple fact is that they sound good—*really good*. Eric Clapton, Stevie Ray Vaughan, Jimi Hendrix, Jimmy Page, Jeff Beck, John McLaughlin, Eric Johnson, B.B. King, Robben Ford, and many others have made extensive use of pentatonic scales throughout the history of the electric guitar, each achieving inimitable results.

In this book, we're going to discover why the pentatonic scale has been a staple of so many guitarists' vocabulary for so long. Though some pentatonic licks have been recycled throughout the years by many different players, each one has managed to make the scale their own, coloring it with personal nuances and idiosyncrasies. By the time you reach the end of this book, you'll hopefully realize the boundless potential that this scale possesses. The interpretation and application of the pentatonic scale is limited only by your imagination. Sounds serious, huh? It's not; it's fun. Let's get started.

How to Use this Book

The material in this book is presented in order of complexity from simplest to most difficult. It is recommended that you become thoroughly familiar with each chapter before progressing to a new one, as the material builds upon previously learned concepts throughout the book.

Each chapter includes several exercises and typical licks to help you become familiar with each new scale form that is introduced. At the end of each chapter (with the exception of *The Other Scale Forms*), a section entitled *Applied Techniques* will demonstrate these concepts in a full band setting, allowing you to hear how these ideas can be applied to actual musical situations in several different styles.

On the accompanying audio, most examples are played twice: once at normal tempo, and once slower for closer examination. For the *Applied Techniques* tracks, the featured guitar parts are panned hard left, while the rhythm instruments are panned hard right. By adjusting the balance control, you can completely remove the featured part, allowing you to play over the backing tracks yourself. Track 90 contains tuning notes for reference.

About the Recording

Guitars: Chad Johnson
Drums: Lance Ogletree
Bass: Erik Shieffer

Recorded at Famous Beagle Studios in Plano, TX.

What is a Pentatonic Scale?

The word *pentatonic* tells us quite literally the defining characteristic of the scale. It consists of five tones. While technically *any* scale consisting of five tones is a pentatonic one, the name has come to be identified with usually one of two types: the *major pentatonic* scale and the *minor pentatonic* scale. These will be the subject of our study in this book.

Let's begin with the construction of the major pentatonic. As mentioned, the pentatonic is a five-note scale. We can build a major pentatonic by omitting the 4th and 7th degrees of a major scale. So the intervallic construction of a major pentatonic scale would be 1–2–3–5–6, as demonstrated below.

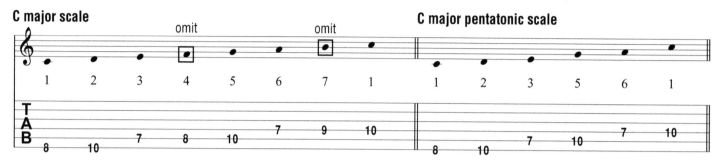

Now let's look at a minor pentatonic. We construct a minor pentatonic by omitting the 2nd and 6th degrees of a minor scale. So the intervallic construction of a minor pentatonic scale would be 1–♭3–4–5–♭7, as demonstrated below.

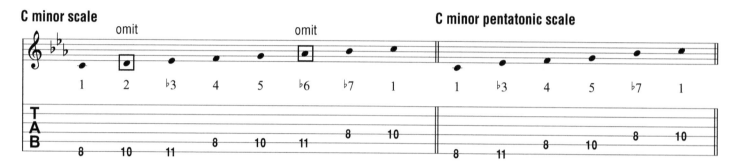

Essentially, the chord/scale relationship that exists with major and minor scales exists with pentatonics as well. If you're playing over a progression in which all the chords belong to C major, for example, you could use a C major scale or a C major pentatonic scale over the whole progression; they would both sound great. Likewise, if you were playing over a progression in the key of A minor, both the A natural minor scale and the A minor pentatonic would be safe choices. Let's listen to the C major scale and the C major pentatonic against a C chord to hear the difference:

You may have noticed that, while the 4th (F) and 7th (B) tones of the major scale sound somewhat dissonant, the pentatonic contains all relatively "safe" notes.

The Relative Minor Concept

It's very important to realize the relationship between a major key and its *relative minor key,* as this concept is fundamental throughout this book. If you're familiar with this relationship already, you can move ahead. If not, you'll need to understand it before you proceed.

We can determine a relative minor key by finding the 6th tone of a major scale. In C major, for example, we can count through the notes and find that A is the 6th tone: C(1)–D(2)–E(3)–F(4)–G(5)–A(6). So we say that A minor is the *relative minor* of C major. Any major scale and its corresponding relative minor scale contain the exact same notes—they just begin and end on different ones. This is demonstrated below.

C major pentatonic scale   **A minor pentatonic scale**

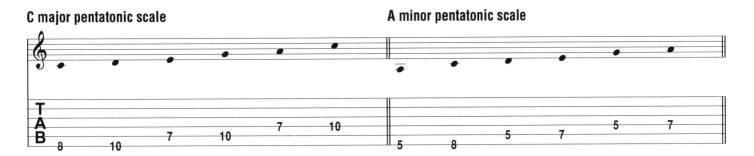

So when you're playing an A minor pentatonic scale, you're really playing the same notes as a C major pentatonic. The only difference that you need to be concerned about is which notes to give more weight to. This is determined by the chord progression underneath. If the progression is in A minor (i.e. A minor is the tonic chord), you would think of the scale as an A minor pentatonic. If the progression were in C major (i.e. C is the tonic chord), you would think of it as C major pentatonic.

The reason that I point this out is so you don't waste time learning something you already know. You don't need to learn all twelve major pentatonics *and* all twelve minor pentatonics over the whole guitar neck. You only need to learn one or the other, because of this relationship. If, for example, you know an A minor pentatonic scale over the entire guitar neck (which you hopefully will by the end of this book), then you know C major pentatonic over the entire neck as well; they are the same scale. The only difference, as mentioned before, is in the way you treat the notes of the scale. We'll examine this difference a little bit later.

Since it is more common in the guitar world to think in terms of minor pentatonic scales, we'll be calling the scales by their minor names for most of this book. A chart is provided below for reference listing all twelve major keys and their relative minor keys.

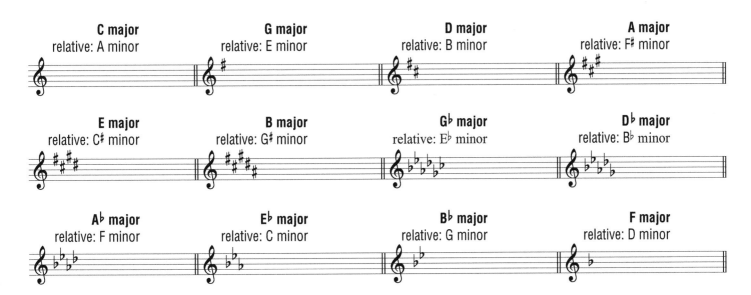

The Basics

Now that we understand the concept of relative minors, let's learn how to play the minor pentatonic scale. Below we'll find the fingering for A minor pentatonic:

TRACK 3

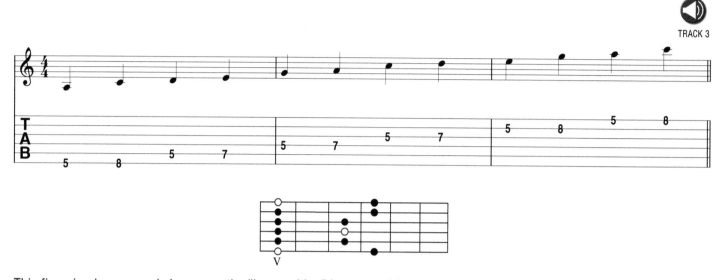

This fingering is commonly known as the "box position" because of the way it resembles a box shape on the fretboard. This is by far the most common pentatonic scale shape on the guitar, and many complete solos have been recorded without budging from this shape. As with any scale shape on the guitar, this shape is moveable. This means that if you want to play in, say, B minor instead of A minor, all you have to do is move the shape up one whole step (two frets) and you've got a B minor pentatonic scale. Move up a minor 3rd (three frets) and you've got a C minor pentatonic, etc. See below:

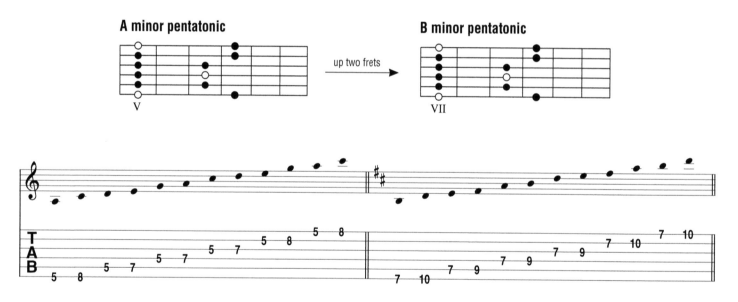

Here we descend through the shape four strings at a time, starting on a lower string each time. You'll have to skip a string at the beginning of each measure, so start slowly and make sure you're picking each note cleanly. I recommend strict alternate picking (down-up-down-up) throughout these exercises. For simplicity, all the exercises in this book will appear in the key of A minor. The typical licks and applied techniques sections will cover different keys.

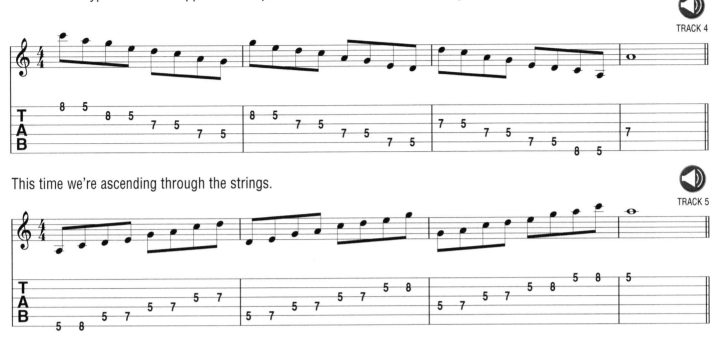

TRACK 4

This time we're ascending through the strings.

TRACK 5

Here a four-note sequence is used to descend through the scale shape. This exercise presents several new problems. Firstly, you're going to encounter every possible picking combination between two strings—remember to maintain consistent alternate picking. Secondly, you'll have to finger the same fret on a different string with the same finger. In measure 1, beat 2 for instance, you'll need to "roll" your first finger from the E note on string 2 to the A note on string 1. This may feel uncomfortable at first, but it really does need to be mastered, as it presents itself time and time again in many licks you'll learn. This happens again at the beginning of measure two. This time, however, your third finger will need to perform the rolling action. It should be noted that some players prefer to use their fourth finger in this instance to catch the D note (first note of measure 2). You can experiment to see which method feels more comfortable. I find myself employing both methods, depending on the situation.

TRACK 6

Now we'll reverse directions and ascend through the sequence. Notice that, in order to roll your first finger from the G note at the end of beat 2 to the D note at the beginning of beat 3 in measure 1, you'll need to fret the G note more on the cushion of your finger (as if you were making a finger print) rather than the tip. This will enable you to roll onto the tip to fret the D note.

TRACK 7

It's very common to bend notes in the pentatonic scale, and here we'll see several examples of the most frequently bent notes. Our first example involves bending the D note on string 3 up to an E. Bending will take quite a bit of getting used to if you're not practiced at it. In order to make sure you're getting the bend in tune, use the E note on the second string (fret 5) as a reference pitch. First play the unbent note on the second string, then bend the third string note to match the pitch. It should also be noted that most players support their third finger with their first and second fingers behind it when bending notes. This will make bending much easier and provide greater control.

TRACK 8

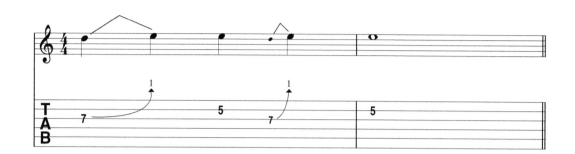

Here we're bending the G note on string 2 up to an A. You can either use your third or fourth finger.

TRACK 9

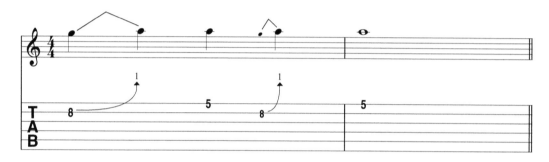

And now we bend the C note on string 1 up to a D.

TRACK 10

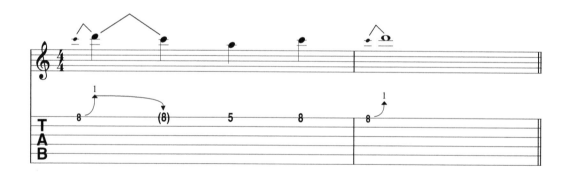

This lick combines all three bends. Notice the release of the bend in measure 3. This is not picked.

TRACK 11

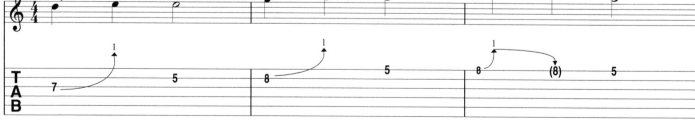

Now that you've gotten familiar with the sound and fingering of this scale, let's apply it to actual music. We mentioned before that A minor pentatonic and C major pentatonic contain the same notes, and the only difference between them lies in the melodic treatment of the notes. Let's take a look now specifically at that difference. Below are two musical examples in which the progressions are identical except for one chord. In the first example, the chord progression begins and ends on a C chord, thus placing the progression in the key of C major. Notice how the phrase resolves on the note C at the end.

TRACK 12

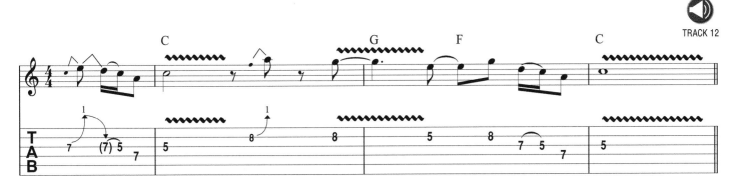

In this next example, the chord progression begins and ends on Am, thus placing it in the key of A minor (the relative minor of C major). Notice that, with the exception of the final note, the exact same phrase is played. The only difference is that we end the phrase on the note A.

TRACK 13

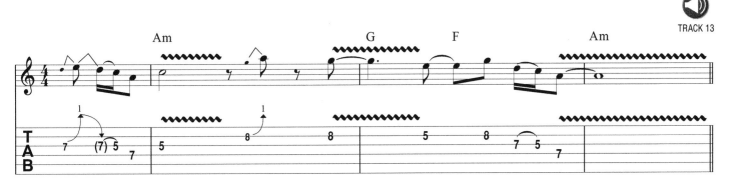

This is not to say that any time you're playing C major pentatonic, you must end on the note C, and any time you're playing A minor pentatonic, you must land on A. It's just to demonstrate that the relationship of the notes will change depending on the chords beneath them—but they're still the same notes. The two scales are played the same way, and your fingers don't know the difference. Your brain, however, does know the difference, and it's the one telling your fingers to stress different notes at different times.

So, now you've got this great scale under your fingers, and you're ready to put it to use. Let's learn a few typical box-position pentatonic licks so we can see what this scale can do. The first bend here, from the 4th (D) to the 5th (E), is probably the most common pentatonic bend of all. The second bend is a quarter-step bend. This is simply a bluesy touch that is common in many styles. The exact pitch is not as important here, as you're going for an in-between-the-notes vibe anyway. It just provides a little sass.

TRACK 14

Pay special attention to the staccato marks in this lick; they lend variety to the phrase and help keep things interesting.

TRACK 15

Here we're in C minor pentatonic and make use of the quarter-step bend in two different octaves. Notice the mixture of picked notes and pulled off notes. While picking every note has its place, a combination of picked notes and legato ones usually lends a musical quality to the phrase. It also helps to break up the monotony a bit.

TRACK 16

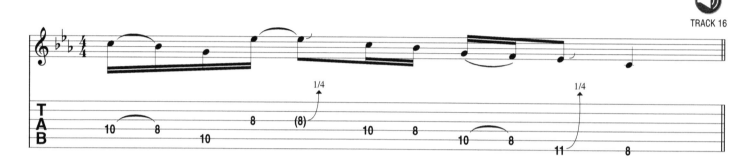

This lick, in D minor, illustrates a time-tested pentatonic favorite. Notice the syncopation created within this phrase. Many times, this grouping of three is repeated over and over, creating great rhythmic interest.

TRACK 17

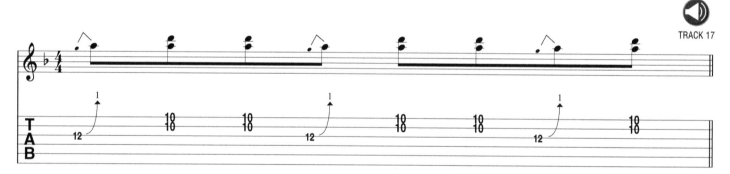

Applied Techniques

Now let's hear some of these pentatonic phrases in some actual musical contexts. This lick in A illustrates an important concept: it can actually sound good to play *A minor pentatonic* over an *A major chord*. This minor-major tension results in a bluesy sound that has been a mainstay for years in the guitar world. Early rock 'n' rollers like Chuck Berry and Eddie Cochran made extensive use of this sound, and blues players from B.B. King to Stevie Ray Vaughn have followed suit.

Rock 'n' Roll

TRACK 18

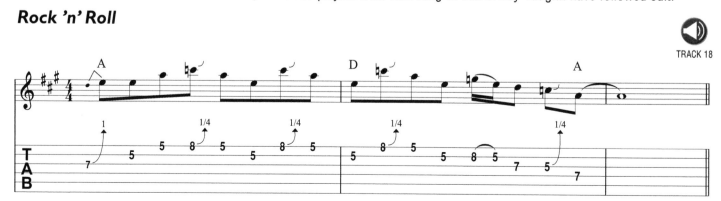

The pentatonic scale can be used to create quick, repeating phrases useful in building momentum. This metal-approved lick in G minor culminates in the final bent F note of the fourth measure. Notice that this note is treated to a healthy dose of vibrato. Adding vibrato to a bent note will require some practice, but it's well worth it. The technique is used in many styles, including blues, rock, metal, country, and fusion to name a few. To achieve this effect, simply release the bend slightly and then push it back up. Repeat this quickly over and over.

Metal

TRACK 19

Here we find a typical pentatonic blues lick that is perfectly suited for the solo break at the end of a 12-bar blues. This particular licks occurs at measure 11 of the progression. The audio begins with one measure of A7 (V) and one measure of G7 (IV) in order to hear the lick in context (not shown in the music). This would be the equivalent of beginning in measure 9 of a 12-bar progression. Notice the quarter-step bends throughout.

Blues

TRACK 20

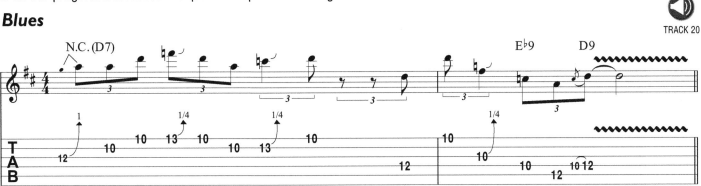

This C minor fusion lick treats the pentatonic scale to a more angular approach, demonstrating how the many inherent 4th intervals of the pentatonic scale can be exploited to create a less typical sound for the guitar. Be sure you're playing all of these notes cleanly and not allowing them to ring together. I find myself using fingers 3 and 2 for the F–C notes (on strings 3 and 4) in beat 3, measure 1 and beat 2, measure 2 as opposed to rolling my third finger to catch both of them. See what works best for you.

Fusion

TRACK 21

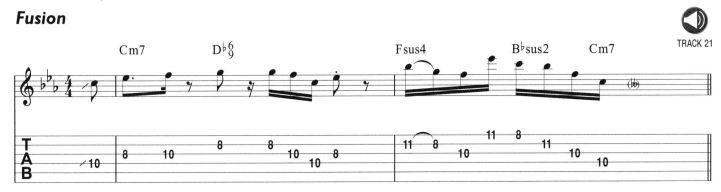

Extended Box Shape

By now, you should be getting fairly familiar with the standard pentatonic box shape. So let's raise the bar a bit and learn a common extension of this shape. This five-note shape presents a whole new world of licks and possibilities and serves great purpose in any guitarist's bag of tricks. Here's the shape:

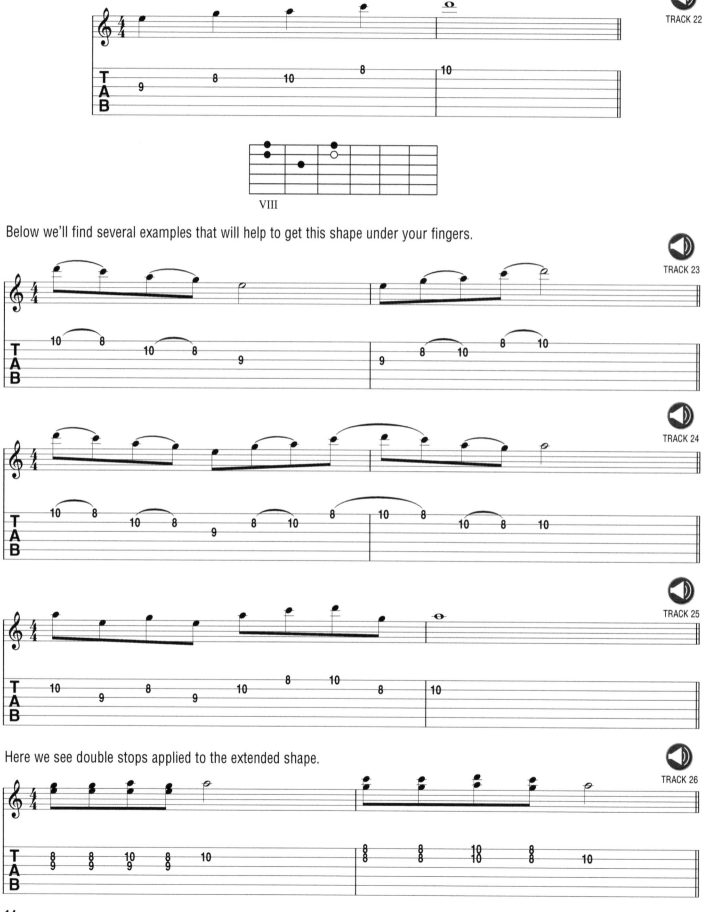

Below we'll find several examples that will help to get this shape under your fingers.

Here we see double stops applied to the extended shape.

This is a classic blues move in this shape. If the tempo is not too fast, the double stops in this type of lick are usually performed with either all downstrokes or all upstrokes for consistency in tone.

TRACK 27

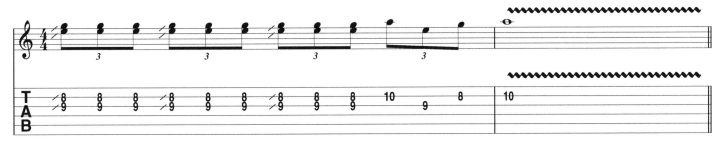

Notice the question-and-answer phrasing in this example. This is a common device used to provide direction to a solo. I'll usually pick this type of double-stop lick with all downstrokes as well.

TRACK 28

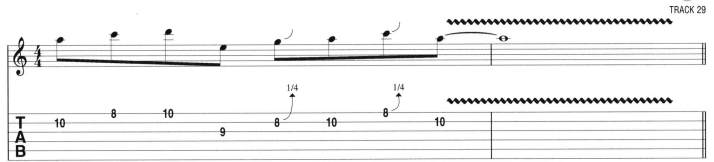

Try this one without the quarter-step bends to hear the difference. It's a subtle effect, but you'd notice it if it weren't there.

TRACK 29

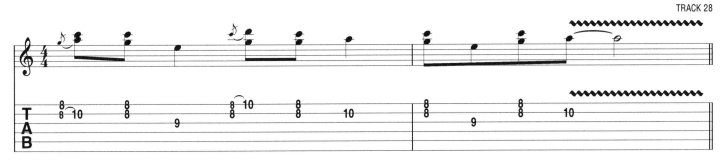

This lick makes a great picking exercise if you begin with a downstroke. Don't let the notes ring together.

TRACK 30

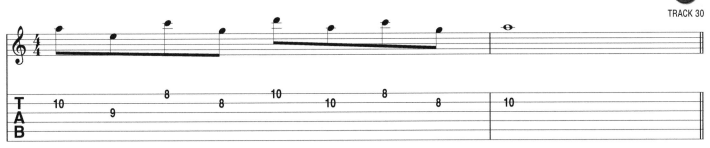

Here we see a keyboard-like phrase using this shape. Remember to roll your first finger when moving from the C notes on string 1 to the G notes on string 2.

TRACK 31

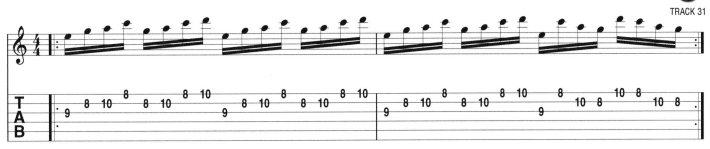

In this example, a syncopated riff on strings 1 and 2 is imitated on strings 2 and 3. The phrase rounds out in beats 3 and 4 of measure 2. I finger the lick 3–1–2, 3–1–2 to avoid the notes ringing together.

TRACK 32

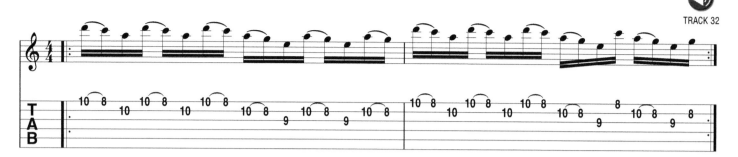

Here's a very common blues lick using this shape. Be sure to dig in to get that blues attitude.

TRACK 33

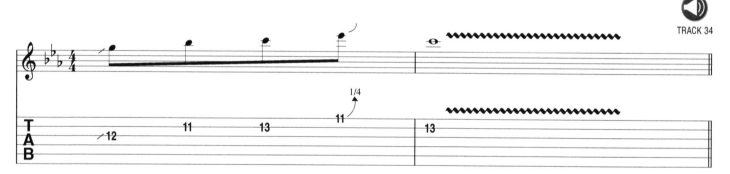

In this example we see the shape applied to a blues lick in C. Don't neglect the slide and quarter-step bend; they are essential to the sound. This lick makes a great intro to a song or a solo.

TRACK 34

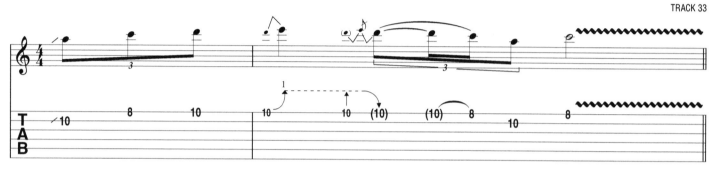

This lick in G minor makes use of the staccato technique once again. Notice how it lends more weight to the final G note. As a nice variation to this lick, try replacing the staccato note with an eighth-note rest.

TRACK 35

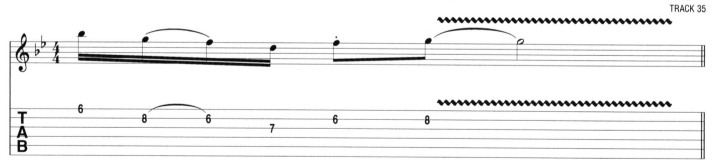

Applied Techniques

In these next few examples, we'll learn how the standard box shape can be connected to the extended shape in one continuous phrase. Our first example, a brooding R&B-style lick in A minor, makes use of just about every expressive technique we've seen thus far: slides, whole-step bends, quarter-step bends, pull-offs, staccato, and vibrato. The first three notes of measure 2 (E–G–A) can be fingered with either 3–2–4 or 2–1–3.

TRACK 36

R&B

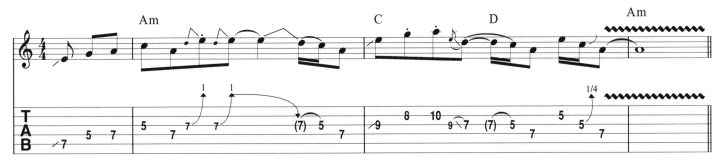

Every note of of this fusion lick is picked, lending a machine-like synth vibe to the line. Notice again the abundance of 4ths; this is typical of the fusion sound.

TRACK 37

Fusion

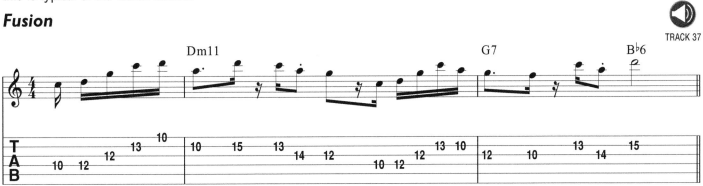

Here we see is a straight-ahead rock lick in C minor. Notice that measure 1 is similar to Track 17. This is a common variant on the lick. Also take note of the use of pull-offs and slides throughout this lick. They're not only there for musical reasons; they facilitate the execution of such licks at this tempo.

TRACK 38

Rock

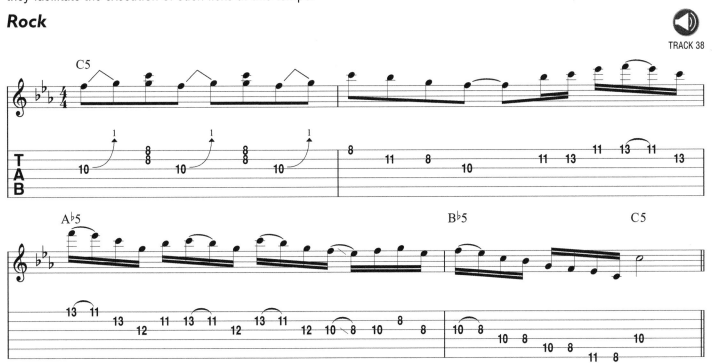

The Other Scale Forms

If you were to quit right now with the knowledge you've gained thus far, you'd know as much as many fine players. Certain-ly, countless solos have been recorded within the confines of the standard box shape and extended box shape. The fact that you bought this book, however, probably means you want to learn as much as you can about the pentatonic scale. This means, among other things, learning the scale over the entire neck. So let's proceed now with the four remaining scale forms.

Second Scale Form

Below we find the fingering for the second form in A minor pentatonic, which begins on the note C. Two things about this scale should be noted. Firstly, this form is simply the continuation of the extended box shape we learned in the previous chapter. All we've done is continue the scale down the remaining strings. Secondly, this form would also go by another name. Can you guess what it is? You guessed it—the C major pentatonic scale. (I told you they were the same scale!)

TRACK 39

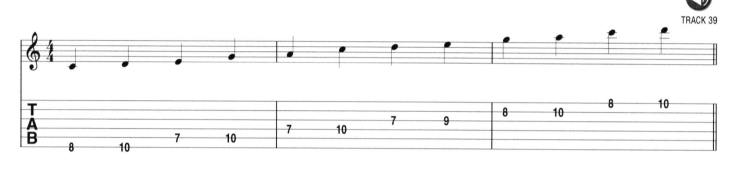

VII

This example should help to get this form under your fingers. Remember to roll your first finger for the seventh-fret string crossings. It should be noted that most players prefer to use fingers 1 and 3 for the top two strings in this form, even though one-finger-per-fret logic would dictate fingers 2 and 4.

TRACK 40

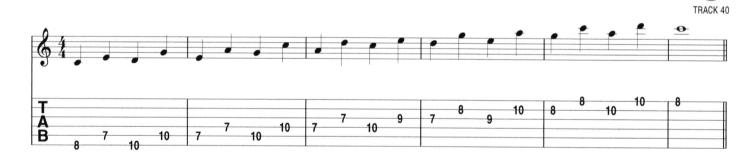

Here we ascend through the form using double stops. I prefer to use fingers 3 and 4 for the tenth fret in measure 1. You could also barre your third finger if you'd like.

TRACK 41

This example consists of a four-note ascending sequence repeated throughout the scale form. This form presents several fingering concerns. From beat 1 to beat 2 in measure 1, for example, logic would dictate that we should roll our fourth finger from the G note on string 5 to the D note on string 6. Many players find this rolling motion difficult with their fourth finger because it's so much shorter than the third finger. I am definitely one of those players. To get around this, I'll finger the G note with my fourth finger and then stretch a little bit with my third finger to catch the D note. I use this same technique when moving from the C note in beat 3 to the G note in beat 4. Experiment and see which method feels best to you. If rolling your fourth finger feels good, go for it.

TRACK 42

Here we see a slight variation to the descending four-note pentatonic sequence. The angular sound of this type of sequence can be used to great effect when wanting to shake things up a bit. Try beginning this phrase on different sixteenth notes for a really interesting rhythmic effect.

TRACK 43

This example presents a typical triplet lick in A minor. Note the specific placement of pull-offs; they make the job for your right hand much easier and allow the lick to breathe a bit.

TRACK 44

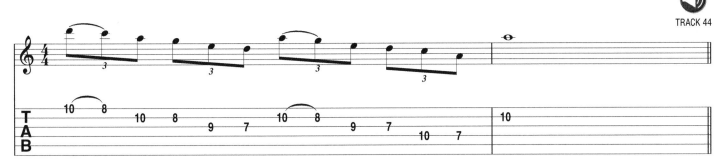

Here's an alternative fingering for a typical blues lick in C minor. This lick could be fingered in the standard box position (with different pull-offs), but this scale form lends a different sound to the notes. This lick should sound familiar; it's Track 16 transposed up an octave.

TRACK 45

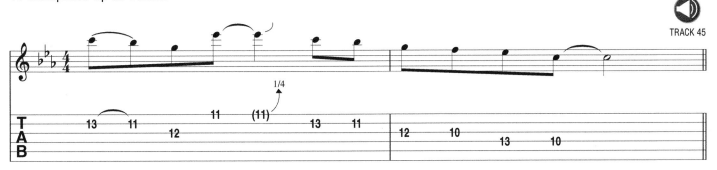

Third Scale Form

So far, so good? Ok. It's time for the third form, which begins on D. This is the only form that spans more than four frets. This will require a slight shift moving from string 3 to string 2.

TRACK 46

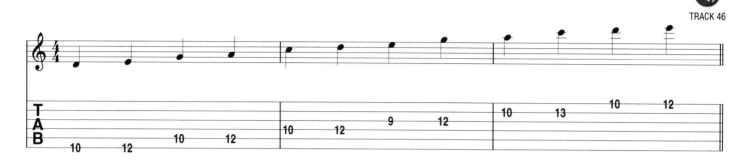

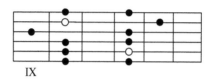

IX

Here we see a variant on the sequence we learned in Track 43. You may have to experiment with the fingering on this one to see what feels best for you. I've included the fingering that I use. If it doesn't work for you, feel free to find something better suited to your style.

TRACK 47

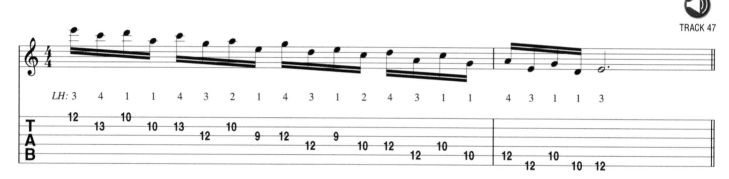

Here we're descending and ascending through the scale form, but with a twist. I've included my fingering with this one as well, as it presents a few difficulties.

TRACK 48

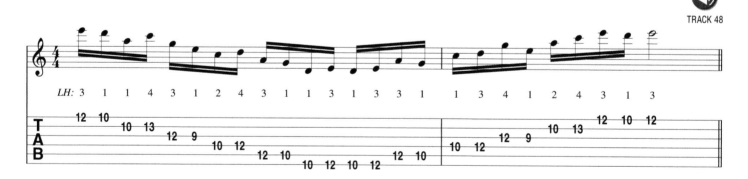

Many riffs have been built from this scale form. This example in F minor repeats an octave higher in measure 2. Notice how the placement of the hammer-ons slightly changes the feel in the second measure.

TRACK 49

Double stops are applied to this syncopated riff in E minor. Don't leave out the slide at the end of measure 1; it's an important part of the sound.

TRACK 50

This typical lick in F♯ minor could just as easily be performed in the standard box position. The tone in this scale form is thicker though, whereas the box form would result in a more stinging tone. Again, the pull-off serves the dual purpose of breaking up the monotony and facilitating speed.

TRACK 51

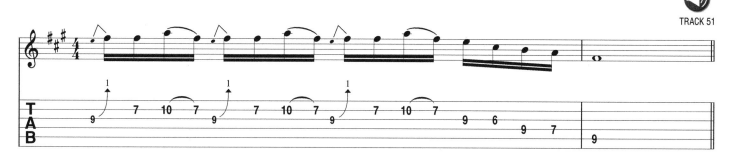

Here's a line in D minor that emphasizes strict alternate picking. Notice that the momentum gained by the first three beats is resolved by a consequent phrase in beat 4. This gives the phrase a sense of conclusion rather than just repeating the same figure four times.

TRACK 52

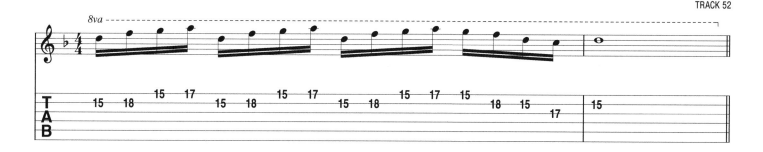

Fourth Scale Form

Moving on, we come to the fourth scale form, which begins on E. This shape closely resembles the standard box shape, so be sure to not get them confused.

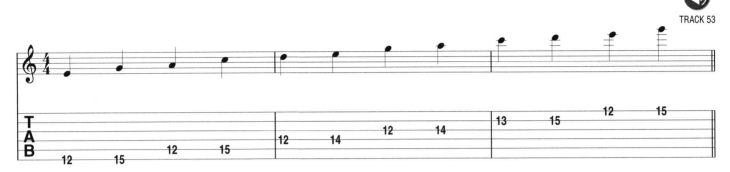

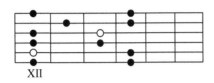

Here we see an eighth-note sequence descending through the scale form. Again, watch the fingering and make sure you're not allowing the notes to ring together.

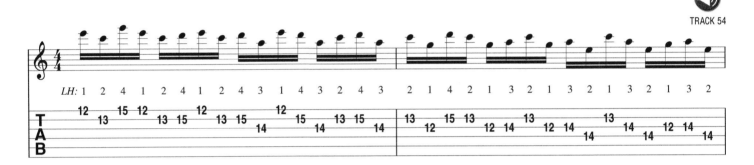

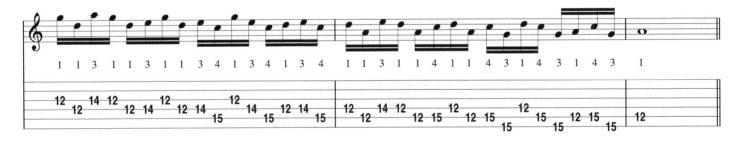

In this exercise, not only are we skipping strings throughout, we're also alternating melodic direction.

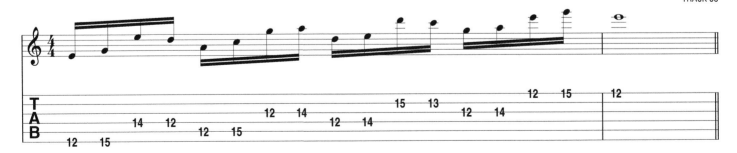

This example in D minor ascends through the entire scale form using double stops. A number of fingerings are possible here; experiment and see what feels best for you.

TRACK 56

The grace note-bends in this F# minor lick lend an Eastern flavor to this example. Obviously, on the lower strings you'll need to pull the string down instead of pushing it up to achieve the bends. This may feel awkward at first, but you'll get the hang of it in no time.

TRACK 57

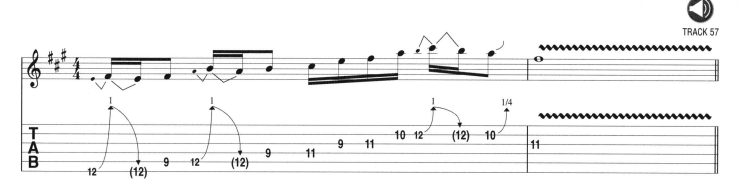

Here's a classic bending lick in A minor. You'll need to bend the D note with your third finger (again, supported by your first and second) and catch the high G note with your fourth finger.

TRACK 58

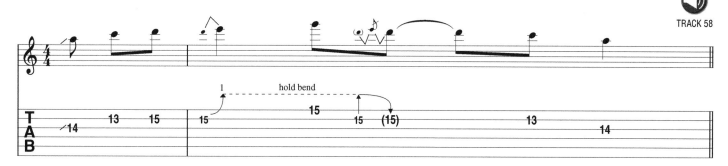

In this E minor lick, the G note on string 2 is bent a quarter step, while the B note on string 1 remains unbent. This may take a little getting used to, but you'll find that if you were to bend the B as well, it may sound a little sour.

TRACK 59

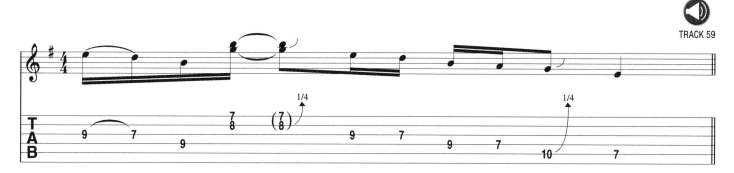

23

Fifth Scale Form

Finally, we come to the fifth and last scale form, which begins on G.

TRACK 60

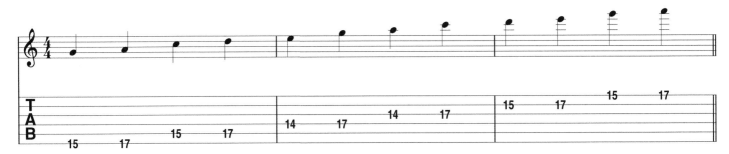

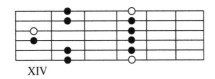

XIV

This example ascends through the entire form in double stops. Again, there are several fingering possibilities here, but I think it's safe to say that most players would barre the first double stop of each measure with their first finger.

TRACK 61

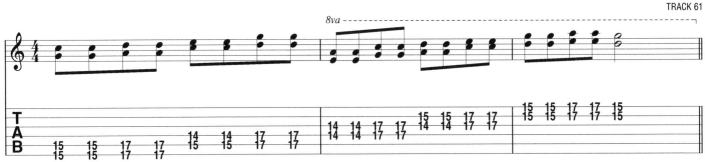

Here we see a one-and-a-half step bend. You'll really need to support the bending finger on this one. Notice how the same rhythmic figure in beats 2 and 3 is phrased differently with the pull-offs placed in different spots.

TRACK 62

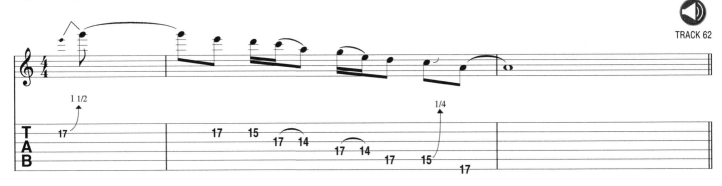

Here's yet another four-note descending sequence. This time however, instead of descending straight through four consecutive notes each time, we descend through three notes and then skip one for the fourth note. This gives the sequence a different flavor and, once again, presents some fingering problems. I've listed my fingering for a starting point.

TRACK 63

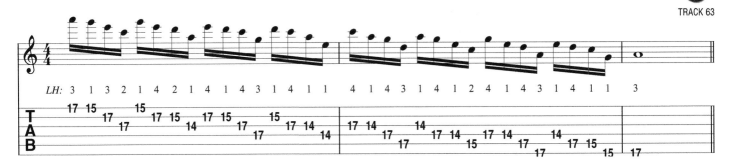

This time we ascend the scale in the form of an eight-note ascending-descending sequence. I've included my fingering for this one as well.

TRACK 64

Try this familiar lick without the pull-offs and notice the difference in tone. This one provides a good opportunity to make use of your fourth finger if you tend to rely on your third finger for much of your bending. The G string at this part of the neck is fairly easy to bend.

TRACK 65

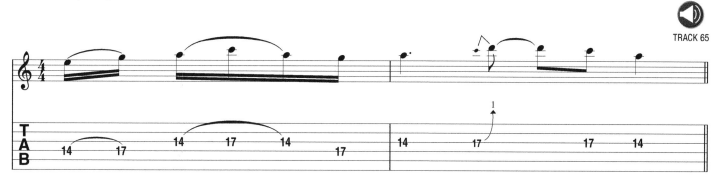

With its ringing quality and repeating motive, this G minor lick has a southern rock flair to it. Keep the first finger barred across the first two strings. This three-on-four type of rhythmic syncopation is extremely common in this style.

TRACK 66

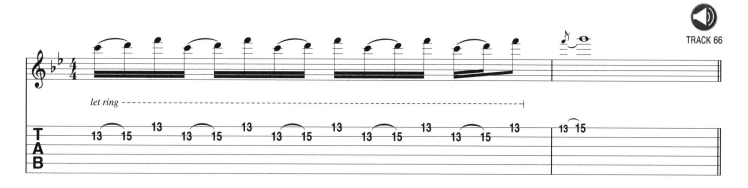

Breaking the Position-Playing Barrier

Ok. So you've learned all your pentatonic scale forms, and you've got them all under your fingers. You can play several different licks in several different positions on the neck without having to think for twenty minutes to do it. What's left?

The true benefit in knowing all these forms is in the freedom it provides—freedom to move seamlessly from one position to the next without having to think about it. Have you ever stared at a player in awe as he spanned the entire neck in one lick? Well, in this chapter, you're going to learn how to do just that. Before we jump in though, let's make sure you're solid on all the forms.

This lick incorporates all five forms of the A minor pentatonic scale in one non-stop lick. If you've fudged your way through any of the forms so far, it's going to show now.

TRACK 67

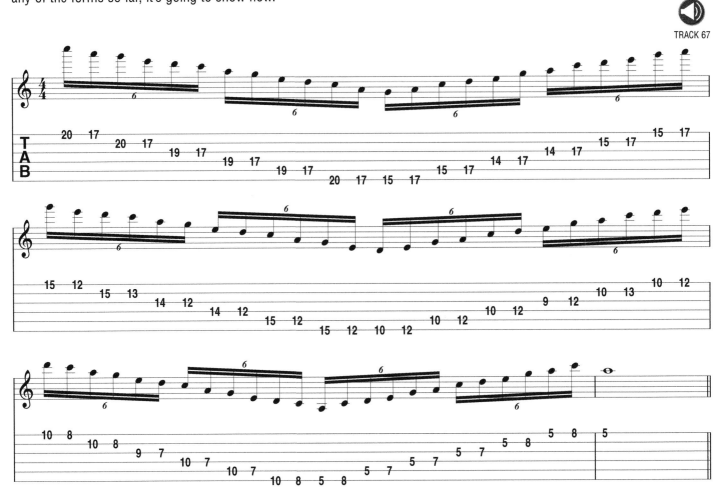

Here we see the same figure played with only one difference. The first phrase features a third-finger slide from A to C, while the second phrase features a first-finger slide from G to A. This is done to demonstrate that there are a number of ways to connect two scale forms together. Different situations, such as personal preference, ease of execution, or musical logic will dictate which one works best for you.

TRACK 68

This example moves through one scale form each beat by way of slides until you reach your destination—one full octave above where you started. You'll find slides invaluable when moving between different scale forms.

TRACK 69

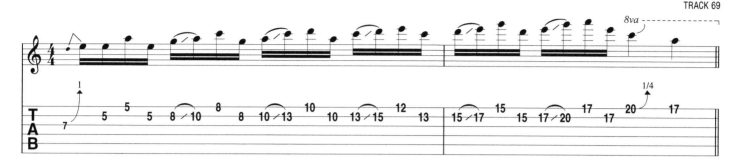

This example accomplishes this one-octave climb by way of shifts and strict alternate picking.

TRACK 70

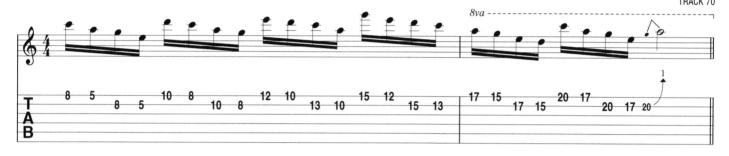

Here is an impressive "span the neck" lick that climbs from the A note on fret 5 of string 6 to the C note on fret 20 of string 1. Note the extensive use of slides. The trick here is to be able to stress the three-note groups as sixteenths instead of triplets.

TRACK 71

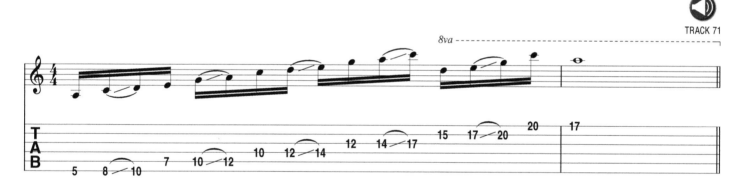

Applied Techniques

This rock lick in Em begins in standard position at fret 12 and ends up in the third scale form at fret 5. I use my second finger on the A note at the beginning of beat 4. The rest of the lick falls into place after that.

Rock

TRACK 72

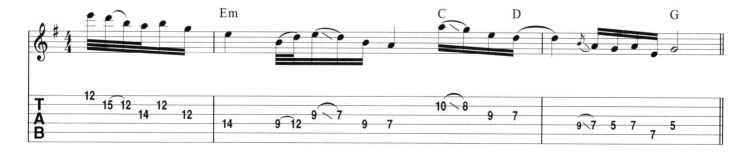

This C blues lick will require a few position shifts, but they all occur after long, sustained notes so they shouldn't pose a problem. This one is played without a pick. Try to really pop the notes to mimic the sound on the audio.

Blues Rock

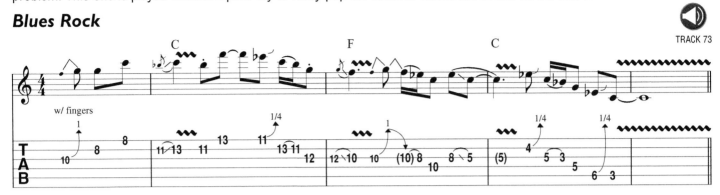

This lick begins at the tenth-fret standard D minor pentatonic form, but it doesn't stay there for long. After a few melodic phrases, it launches into a sixteenth-note phrase that weaves down through four scale forms before ending on the tonic D note. Again, note the use of slides as a transition device. Pull-offs play a vital role in the sound and playability of this lick as well.

Rock

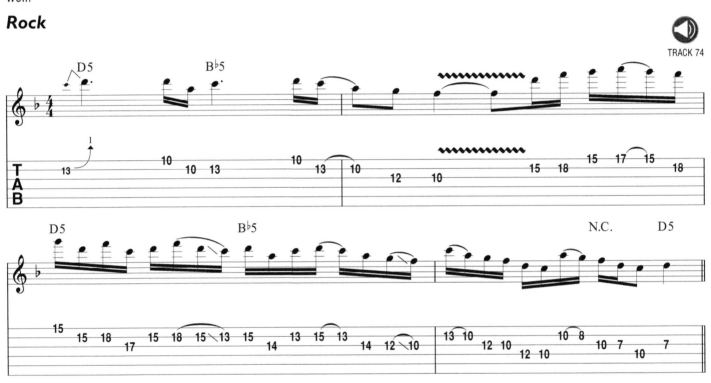

This fusion example is all about making it legato. With the exception of four or five notes, every note is either slid to/from, hammered, or pulled off. This phrase demonstrates how a pentatonic scale can be a very colorful choice when set against less typical chords.

Fusion

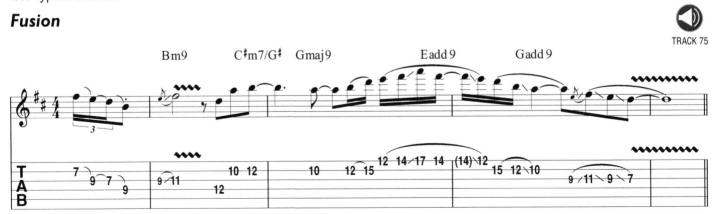

Pentatonic Substitution Ideas

Athis point, you should be fairly comfortable with the fingerings of the pentatonic scale over the whole of the guitar neck. Before we move any further, let's take a second to review what we've learned so far.

1) We can apply a major or minor pentatonic scale to any situation that we would normally apply a major or natural minor scale. For instance, if we're playing in the key of D major, we could use a D major pentatonic scale or a D major scale, and they will both sound fine. If we're playing in C minor, we could use a C minor pentatonic scale or a C natural minor scale.

2) The relative minor of a major key can be determined by locating the 6th degree of a major scale.

3) The only difference between a major pentatonic scale and its relative minor pentatonic scale is in the treatment of the notes. When you are playing D major pentatonic, you're playing the same notes as B minor pentatonic, and vice versa.

4) Slides and pull-offs can greatly aid in moving between scale forms and executing faster passages.

This brings us to a concept called *substitution*. The basic idea here is to use a pentatonic scale from a different root over a particular chord to access certain notes that you wouldn't normally find in the standard major or minor pentatonic scale. In order to explore this more fully, we need to briefly cover the concept of chord tones and *extensions*. It will be assumed that you are familiar with the spelling of basic chords (triads) for this section. If you are not, you may want to read up on this subject; there are many books dedicated specifically to chord construction.

If we're playing over a C major chord, we've learned so far that we have at least two choices of scales to play: a C major scale (C–D–E–F–G–A–B) and a C major pentatonic scale (C–D–E–G–A). Let's say that we wanted to imply a Cmaj7 sound over the C major chord. The only difference between a basic C triad and a Cmaj7 is the addition of B, the seventh tone of the major scale. So a Cmaj7 chord is spelled C–E–G–B. Knowing this, we can determine that we will not be able to create a Cmaj7 sound with a C major pentatonic scale, because we do not have the B note present. A C major scale does contain a B note, but it also contains notes that we might not want, such as F (the 4th). We could just say, "Ok, I'll just play a C major scale and avoid landing on the F." This is perfectly doable, but there is another method.

If we were to play a minor pentatonic off the 3rd of the C major chord (E), we would end up with E–G–A–B–D. Note that the only difference between this scale and the C major pentatonic is that C is now replaced with B, the major seventh. Let's hear how this sounds. In the following example, we begin in measure 1 with C major pentatonic, but in measure 2 we start playing E minor pentatonic.

TRACK 76

This approach allows you to specifically target the extension tone you want, without having to worry about avoiding other tones in the scale. This idea of scale substitution has basically no limits. You should experiment with different scales over different chords and take note of the ones you like. We'll cover a few possibilities in the next few examples.

Applied Techniques

This rock groove in C minor employs the same substitution principle we just used, except this time we're over an E♭ chord. G minor pentatonic (scale form 4) is substituted over E♭ to access the 7th (D). In measure 3, over the A♭ chord, we switch to F minor pentatonic (scale form 4—remember: this is the same as A♭ major pentatonic!). In measure 4, however, we switch back to C minor pentatonic (scale form 1), which gives us the 7th (G) of A♭. Notice how the G note is sustained on beat 3 to bring out the bright sound of the major 7th.

Rock

TRACK 77

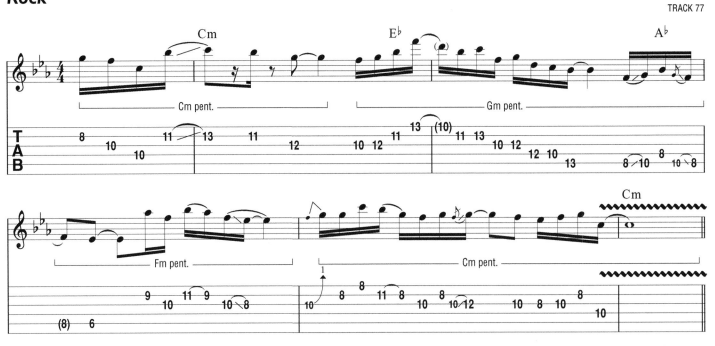

This jazz blues example takes this concept a bit further. We begin with A minor pentatonic (scale form 2) over the C7 chord. The half-step slides are used to provide a bluesy effect. In measure 2, over the F7 chord, we switch to C minor pentatonic (scale form 1). This is because the F7 chord contains the note E♭, and A minor pentatonic contains E♮, which would clash a bit. In measure 3, things get even more interesting. G minor pentatonic (scale form 4) is played over beats 1 and 2, and we switch back to A minor pentatonic (scale forms 3 and 2) for beats 3 and 4. What this does is essentially imply a ii–V (Gm7–C7) progression moving to F in measure 4. This type of ii–V implication is very common in jazzier styles.

Jazz Blues

TRACK 78

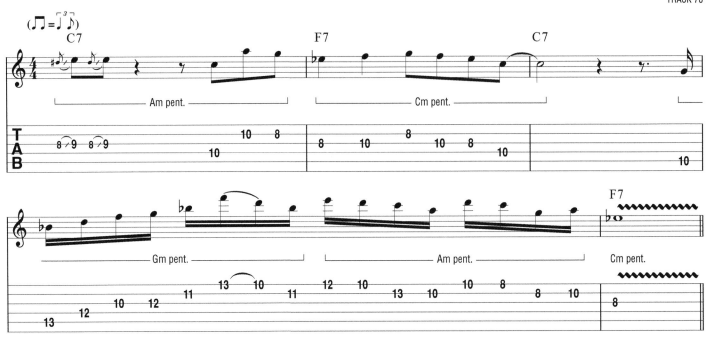

This funk fusion lick begins in E minor pentatonic (scale form 1). In measure two, B minor pentatonic (scale form 3) is played, thus giving us the note F# and creating an Em9 sound (E–G–B–D–F#). The beginning of measure 3 finds us in E minor pentatonic (scale form 1) again. Beats 3 and 4 briefly make use of B minor pentatonic (scale form 4) before returning to E minor pentatonic (scale form 2).

Funk Fusion

TRACK 79

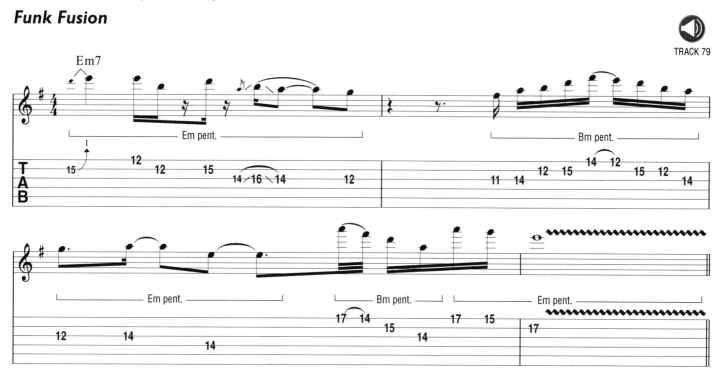

This jazz phrase takes the pentatonic substitution idea way out there. Each chord of this ii–V–I progression in D major receives its own substitution. Over Em7 in measure 1, a B minor pentatonic (scale form 1) descending lick is played. This is the same idea we saw in Track 79—the result is an Em9 sound. In measure 2, things get pretty out there. Over A7♭9#5, we play C minor pentatonic (scale forms 1, 2, and 3). Why? Well let's take a look at our C minor pentatonic scale. We have the notes C–E♭–F–G–B♭. These notes all fit within the A7 altered sound: C is the #9, E♭ is the ♭5, F is the #5, G is the ♭7, and B♭ is the ♭9. Since this scale happens to contain almost all altered notes (the G is the only non-altered tone), it's going to really accent the altered sound of the A7. Finally, in measure 3, we imply a maj7 sound over the D6 chord by playing F#m pentatonic (scale forms 4 and 3).

Jazz

TRACK 80

The Blues Scale

Well, I tried, but I just wasn't able to write a guitar book about pentatonic scales without mentioning the blues scale. Blues and pentatonics go hand in hand so often that I just couldn't leave it out.

Basically, a blues scale is simply a pentatonic scale with one added note. This is the ♭5 (or ♯4). Below, we find the first scale form (standard box shape) for the A blues scale. Note that this shape is exactly the same except for the two added E♭ (D♯) notes.

TRACK 81

Virtually any of the licks in this book could be made into blues scale licks by including this note somewhere. It will give the sound a bit more of a—well—"bluesy" edge to it, but it will sound great. I've included a chart here that shows the scale forms for the A blues scale over the entire neck. You can memorize this, or you can simply go through your pentatonics and insert an E♭ note before every E note.

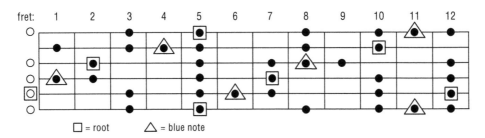

□ = root   △ = blue note

Now let's hear the blues scale in action. Here we see a descending lick making use of the blues scale. Notice that the blues note is used as a passing tone on the weak part of the beat—the last sixteenth note. While it's not unheard of to accent the blues note on a strong beat, many times the strong beats are reserved for more stable tones.

TRACK 82

This example makes use of double stops within the blues scale, creating an organ-type sound. I play this lick fingerstyle to really bring out both voices evenly.

TRACK 83

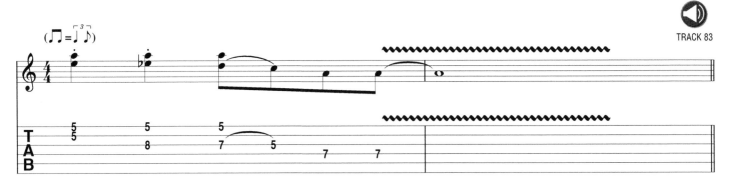

Applied Techniques

This blues in C starts off in the C minor blues box with some bends, slides, and healthy vibrato in measures 1 and 2. In the second half of measure 3, we launch into a one-and-a-half measure sixteenth-note run in scale form 2 that makes use of slides and pull-offs to add fluidity to the line. Notice that the blue note (F#) is only sounded three times in this entire lick, demonstrating that you don't have to grind this note into the ground for it to be heard.

Blues

TRACK 84

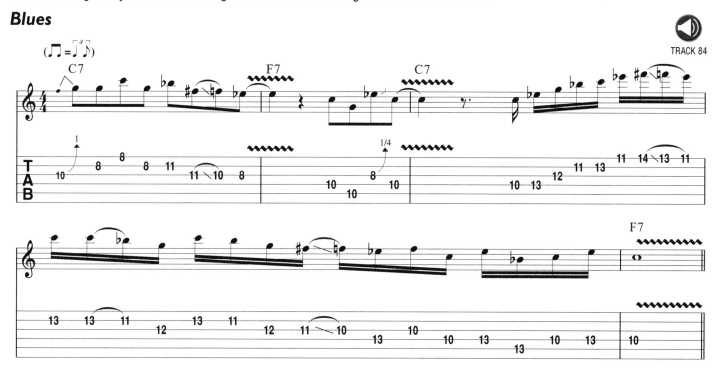

This lick covers a lot of ground. The progression has a G Dorian flavor to it, due to the minor tonic (Gm7) and major IV chord (C/G) relationship. We begin in the pickup measure with a phrase in scale form 3. The blue note here (Db) is actually a very brief grace note, but it's still effective. Measure 2 finds us in the home-base blues box shape, employing legato slides for a smooth sound. In measure 3, we move up to scale form 5 and kick off a descending blues-scale line with a one-and-a-half-step bend. Measure 4 brings things to a close in scale form 4.

Blues Rock

TRACK 85

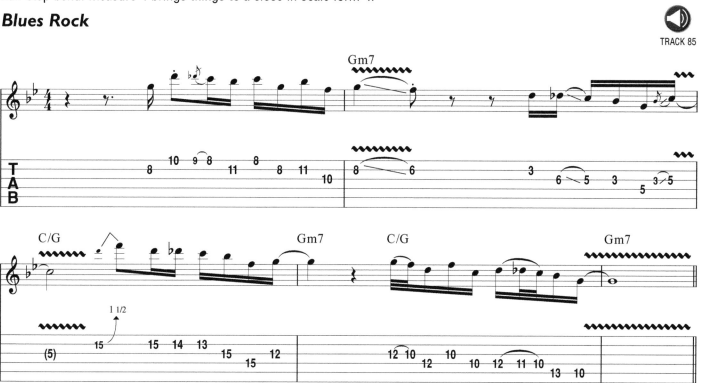

Putting It All Together

This should be the fun section of the book. You've done your homework, learned your scales, practiced them for hours on end (right?), and you're ready to actually play a solo now. Well, here's your chance.

We're finishing things up here with four complete solos that make use of everything we've worked on throughout the whole book. The solos that I've played are transcribed here so you can see these ideas at work in an improvisational context, and the phrases are analyzed to reveal the thought process behind them. This is only half the focus of this section though. The other part is for you to write (or improvise) your own solos. Remember that, by using the balance control on your stereo (or if you don't have a balance control, you could just unplug your left speaker!), you're able to take the lead guitar out of the mix, leaving a wide open rhythm track that's just begging to be soloed over. Let's get on with it.

We start things off with a blues in C. We're soloing over two choruses here, so we have a chance to build up some momentum. In terms of scale usage, this entire solo is nothing but A minor pentatonic (or C major) and C minor pentatonic/blues scale.

We open with a few melodic phrases in A minor pentatonic. In measure 4, we move to C minor pentatonic and remain there through measures 5 and 6 on the IV (F9) chord. Notice the use of slides throughout. Measure 7 finds us in A minor pentatonic again with a few more melodic phrases. Measures 9–12 basically serve one purpose, and that is to build momentum into the second chorus. Comprised of almost entirely triplets, these four measures create a lot of tension that needs to be resolved. This tension is heightened in measure 12 (V) when the same lick is repeated verbatim four times; you know something is about to happen.

The release occurs at the beginning of the second chorus, where we return to melodic, singable phrases in A minor pentatonic that play off the rhythm section hits. This singable section in measures 13–16 is contrasted once again by a long sixteenth-note C blues scale flurry in measures 17 and 18 over the IV chord. Measure 19 finds us briefly back in A minor pentatonic over the I chord. After that, it's all C minor pentatonic and blues, except for the chromatically approached double stop in measure 24; this is a typical blues move.

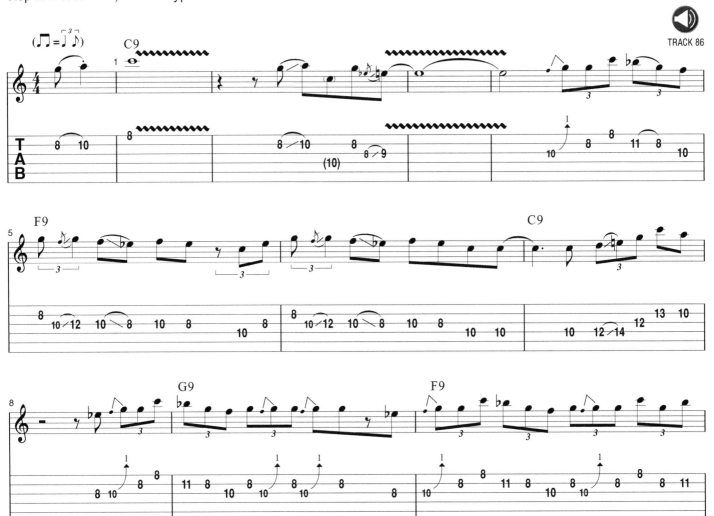

TRACK 86

34

Next we have a dark, swampy groove in A minor. The licks here are more about phrasing and subtlety than flash. We begin with a few sparse melodic statements in A minor pentatonic. In measure 3, we substitute E minor pentatonic to create an Am9 sound. Notice how beat 4 returns to A minor pentatonic. In measure 8, the harmony changes to F9, providing us with an opportunity to use a different sound. The sixteenth-note lick here is based off of the C minor pentatonic scale which gives us the important E♭ note of the F9 chord. In measure 14, we're substituting E minor pentatonic again, but this time over Fmaj7. This provides us with a Lydian sound over the F chord.

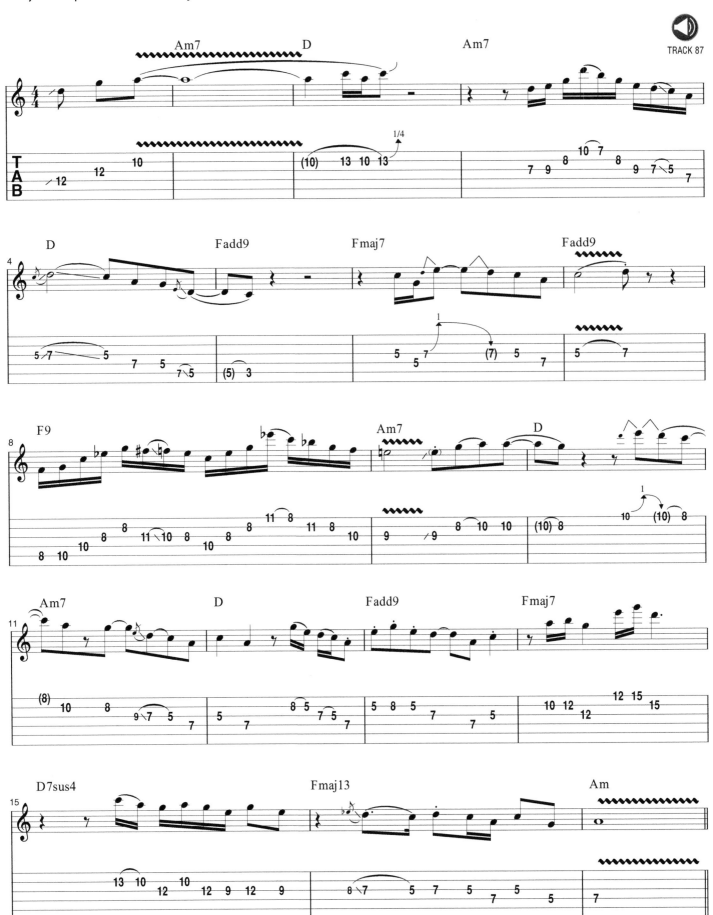

Here we see a full-blown stadium rock tune. The lines here are predominantly based on the D minor pentatonic and B minor (D major) pentatonic scales. We open with some tough bluesy D minor pentatonic licks in measures 1 and 2. Measure 3 introduces the B minor tonality for a brighter sound. This is contrasted in measures 4–6 with some very rhythmically-based D minor blues licks. The effectiveness of phrases like these rests almost entirely in their rhythmic delivery. They've got to be in the pocket in order to really hit home. We get a little flashy in measures 7 and 8 with some sextuplets. The quick ascending run in measure 8 culminates with a high G bent to A that is released in measure 9 with a return to some B minor pentatonic concluding phrases.

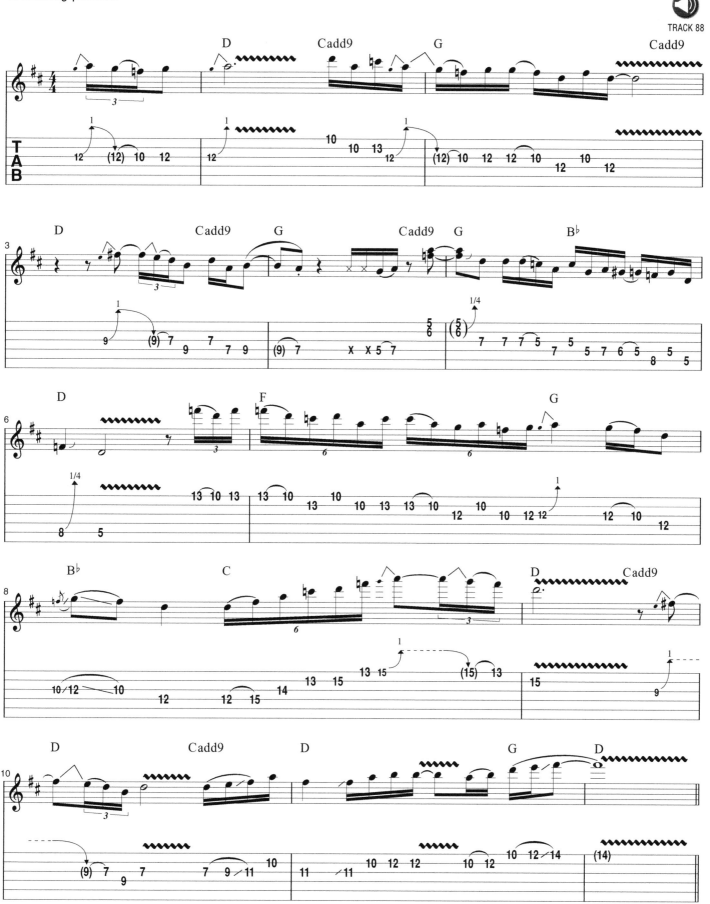

Our last example has a steady, driving rock feel. At thirty-three measures in length, it really gives you a chance to strut your stuff. Measures 1–8 repeat a Dm–Fsus2–B♭ chord progression, and the lines here all come from D minor pentatonic. We're mostly just playing melodies, with one quick little line thrown in for contrast (measure 4). Notice that the major 7th (A) of B♭ is stressed in measure 7. In measure 9, the harmony moves to G7, and the lines here are still based in D minor. We remain there until the new section in measure 13, where we vamp between F and E♭/F. The scale of choice here is C minor pentatonic. This provides us with the E♭, G, and B♭ notes that are present in the E♭ chord. Pay special attention to the sixteenth-note lick that begins in measure 16 and continues through 17. This is a good example of switching pentatonics in the middle of a lick. We ascend in measure 16 in C minor pentatonic, but in measure 17 we're right back in D minor for the second chorus of the solo. In measure 18, we're substituting A minor pentatonic over the F chord for an Fmaj9 sound. We do this again in the midst of a singable melody spanning measures 21 and 22. For the G7–B♭–G7–B♭m progression that follows, we're using imitative phrasing in D minor pentatonic. We wrap things up again in measures 29–33 with C minor pentatonic over the F and E♭/F chords.

Afterword

That wraps it up. Hopefully, you've gained a great understanding of the pentatonic scale, its uses, and some of its possibilities. Remember to put these new ideas to use in your own playing in order to gain the most benefit from this book. Once you become familiar with the concepts in this book, I suggest listening to your favorite players to see if you can identify some of the ideas in their playing. I hope you have found the examples in this book inspiring and enjoyable. Good luck!

About the Author

Chad Johnson studied music at the University of North Texas from 1990–1995. In 1998, he became a senior music editor for iSong.com, an internet-based company that produced instructional guitar-based CDs. After leaving iSong.com in 2000, he began editing, proofing, and authoring books for Hal Leonard. *Pentatonic Scales for Guitar* is the fourth book Chad has written for Hal Leonard Corporation. Currently, Chad resides in Dallas, TX, and keeps busy writing, editing, composing, and recording. For correspondence, write to: chadljohnsonguitar@gmail.com. To keep up with Chad's latest books and other musical projects, check out www.facebook.com/chadjohnsonguitar.